Title: Jesus Was Funnier Than You Think
Subtitle: Unlocking His Wit, Wisdom, and Unexpected Humor
Written by: Christian A. Dickinson
Illustrations by: Learning Engineered LLC
Published by: Learning Engineered Publishing

Library of Congress Control Number: 2025935044
ISBN (Print): 978-1-965741-26-9

First Edition: 2025

Printed & Created in: United States of America
Text and Illustration Copyright © 2025

Learning Engineered Publishing is a division of Learning Engineered LLC and a subsidiary of Carpe Diem Unlimited Holdings, Inc.

LEARNING ENGINEERED
PUBLISHING

Contents

Dedication

To my former teacher, FCA Sponsor, and Coach turned lawyer—**Michael J. Duggar, Esquire.**

The most sarcastic, cynical, satirist, and argumentative Christian I know.
Thank you for sharpening my mind, challenging my beliefs, and proving that faith and wit make an unstoppable combination.

Also, thank you for the endless theological debates—especially the ones where you tried to convince me that free will is an illusion and that I was *predestined* to lose the argument.

— With appreciation and a begrudging nod to your endless Calvinist logic.

Introduction

P icture Jesus at your campfire, winking as He quips,

"Doubts? Even My disciples tripped over planks in their eyes."

You laugh, and His joy sparks yours.

Growing up, I was immersed in the Gospels, surrounded by missionary families whose laughter echoed through our home and lulled me to sleep. Yet the somber portraits of Jesus never matched that joy. I thought holiness meant serious faces—until *The Chosen*, a TV series, showed Jesus laughing, teasing, and engaging His disciples, rekindling memories of a faith alive with warmth.

My friend Nick V. introduced me to *Ante Pacem*, revealing early Christian art of a smiling Jesus—proof that His humor shines in Scripture.

This book traces His wit:
from strategic humor that disarms (Ch. 1),
to teasing disciples like the "Sons of Thunder" (Ch. 2),
absurd planks and camels (Ch. 3),
satirical parables flipping norms (Ch. 4),
and sarcastic jabs at Pharisees (Ch. 5).

As a mathematician, not a theologian, I'm simply spotting patterns in His joy to share with you.

Dive in any way—read straight through or jump to whatever grabs you. Each chapter unpacks His humor, with questions to spark reflection for solo readers, small groups, or sharing your faith.

Scan the QR code for a 6-week Bible study to dig deeper.

My challenge? Read the Gospels afresh, picturing Jesus' grin. You'll find a Savior funnier—and more joyful—than you ever imagined.

Chapter 1

Unpacking the Laughing Messiah

Picture a crackling campfire under a star-lit sky, Jesus and His disciples sprawled around it after a long day of dusty roads and demanding crowds. As the flames dance, Jesus leans in with a sly grin:

"Imagine a guy with a plank jutting out of his eye, squinting to pick a speck from his buddy's. What a clown show!"

Peter snorts. Matthew chuckles, probably picturing a smug Pharisee. Even Judas might crack a smirk before the mood shifts.

We often read this story in Matthew 7:3–5 as a stern warning, but what if it's also a punchline? What if Jesus—the greatest teacher ever—wove humor into His lessons, and we've been too serious to catch it? This quip wasn't just for laughs; it was His genius way of exposing hypocrisy with a smile.

I used to think holiness meant somber faces and heavy hearts. Then I watched *The Chosen*, a TV series showing a Jesus who laughed, teased, and radiated warmth. It rekindled memories of childhood nights when faith felt alive with joy. Turns out, this laughing Messiah isn't Hollywood's invention—it's right there in Scripture, waiting to be seen.

A Savior Who Smiles

We picture Jesus preaching on hills, healing the broken, or weeping in Gethsemane. He did all that. But being fully human also meant joy, laughter, and wit. Kids flocked to Him (Matthew 19:14)—let's be real, they don't swarm a dull teacher. His disciples, a rough crew of fishermen and a tax collector, spent three years on the road with Him. No way that group didn't share laughs.

Early Christian art often showed a smiling, even laughing Jesus, as scholar Graydon Snyder notes. Somewhere along the way, we swapped that joy for a solemn portrait. Yet the Gospels tell a different story. Yes, Isaiah 53:3 calls Him a "man of sorrows," but in John 15:11, Jesus says His joy should fill us—overflowing. He carried the cross and a chuckle.

Jesus' Humor Had a Purpose

Jesus didn't tell jokes for cheap laughs. His humor was sharp, strategic, and soul-deep:

- **Exposed hypocrisy** with wit the self-righteous couldn't dodge.

- **Challenged disciples** with quips that made them squirm, then grow.

- **Engaged doubters** with cleverness that cracked open closed hearts.

- **Made truth stick**—nobody forgets a camel squeezing through a needle's eye.

Take Matthew 7:3–5. The Greek word *dokos* ("plank") means a massive beam, not a twig. Picture a guy with a telephone pole in his eye, trying to perform eye surgery. Ridiculous? That's the point. First-century Jews would've laughed. The Pharisees? Not so much.

Jewish Humor & Exaggeration

Jesus leaned into Jewish humor's love of absurdity to land His point. When He said, "You strain out a gnat but swallow a camel!" (Matthew 23:24), His listeners got the joke. Gnats were tiny, unclean pests; camels were the largest unclean animals. The image? A Pharisee fussing over a speck in his drink while gulping down a camel. Absurd—and brilliant.

Why Humor Hits Home

Science confirms humor makes truth stick, disarms hostility, and builds bonds—Jesus mastered this. Kids still prove it, flocking to anyone who makes them laugh. For centuries, we've taught faith in serious tones, but maybe we've missed something powerful. Maybe joy and truth go hand in hand.

Holiness Meets Hilarity

Jesus wasn't just a man of sorrows—He was a man of joy, wielding humor like a scalpel of truth. Imagine Him at your church picnic, winking as He teases, "Careful, don't trip over that plank in your eye while grabbing the potato salad!" If He sat with your youth group today, He'd probably poke fun—gently, brilliantly—until you laughed and learned.

Maybe we've been too somber for too long. As we picture Jesus chuckling by that campfire, what does His humor say about how we share faith today? Perhaps it's time to hear the Messiah's chuckle.

Next Up: Exaggeration & Absurdity
Next, we'll dive into Jesus' wildest visu-

als—planks, camels, gnats—where humor meets holy havoc.

Chapter 2

Walking with the Messiah—and Getting Teased

Imagine trailing Jesus for three years—witnessing miracles, dodging crowds, and then, out of nowhere, catching His playful grin as He teases you.

One day, you see Him feed thousands with a few loaves and fish. Hours later, a storm hits, and you're panicking like it never happened. Jesus calms the waves, then smirks:

"Oh, you of little faith..." (Matthew 14:31)

Not a scolding, but a nudge—half chuckle, half challenge.

Jesus wasn't just teaching His disciples; He was bonding with them, stretching their faith with wit. This chapter dives into His playful banter, showing how humor built trust, sparked growth, and made truth stick.

Why Jesus Teased

Good-natured teasing connects and challenges:

- It builds camaraderie—shared laughs forge bonds.

- It sparks growth—a witty nudge pushes you higher.

- It eases tension—humor lightens heavy moments.

Jesus wasn't a humorless taskmaster. He laughed, teased, and used wit to shape His crew. Let's unpack His best moments.

"Oh, You of Little Faith!" (Matthew 14:31, 16:8)

Picture Peter stepping onto water, then panicking mid-miracle (Matthew 14:31). Or the disciples fretting over food, forgetting Jesus had just fed thousands (Matthew 16:8).

Jesus raises an eyebrow:

"Really, guys? After all you've seen?"

His playful jab was affectionate yet convicting, nudging them to trust more.

Today's version:

"You've seen God show up, but you're stressing again? Oh, you of little faith!"

The "Sons of Thunder" Nickname (Mark 3:17)

Jesus dubbed James and John "Boanerges"—Sons of Thunder—a cheeky nod to their fiery tempers.

When they suggested torching a village (Luke 9:54), you can imagine Jesus chuckling:

"Yup, classic Sons of Thunder."

The nickname wasn't just funny; it shaped them. John, once a hothead, became the Apostle of Love.

Today's version:

"Here come the Thunder Boys, stirring up a storm again!"

The Emmaus Road Playfulness (Luke 24:13–35)

After His resurrection, Jesus met two grieving disciples on the road to Emmaus but played coy:

"What are you talking about?" (Luke 24:17)

They were stunned:

"Are you the only one who hasn't heard about Jesus?"

Suppressing a grin, He probed further:

"Oh? What things?" (Luke 24:19)

He let them pour out their hearts before revealing Himself. It was a divine mic drop—playful, patient, and faith-stirring.

Today's version:

"Who's this Jesus guy? Sounds interesting..."

"You Feed Them—and Catch Some Fish!" (Matthew 14:16; John 21:5)

When thousands were hungry, Jesus told His disciples:

"You give them something to eat." (Matthew 14:16)

He knew they had just a few loaves.

Later, as they fished in vain, He called out:

"Caught anything?" (John 21:5)

He knew full well their nets were empty.

Both times, He let them squirm before delivering miracles—food for thousands and nets overflowing.

It was like a teacher tossing you an impossible task, then winking as He solved it. Jesus stretched their faith with a grin.

Why Jesus' Playfulness Matters

Jesus' teasing built deep bonds, challenged doubts with wit, and showed that holiness includes joy.

Imagine Him at your Bible study, smirking as you fret over a small worry:

"Really? After all you've seen, you're stressed about that?"

His humor wasn't just fun—it transformed His disciples.

As we picture Him chuckling with His crew, what might His playfulness teach us about growing in faith today?

Next Up: The Satire of Jesus in His Parables

Jesus didn't just tease His disciples—He flipped expectations in His parables, exposing self-righteousness with humor and surprise twists.

Chapter 3

The Art of Holy Hyperbole

A Divine Zinger in the Marketplace

Picture a bustling Jerusalem market-place—traders haggling, Roman soldiers patrolling, Pharisees glaring. Jesus steps forward, voice rising:

"You blind guides! You strain out a gnat but swallow a camel!" (Matthew 23:24)

The crowd snickers. Someone snorts. The Pharisees squirm, caught in His zinger.

This wasn't Jesus losing His cool—it was a masterclass in holy hyperbole. His wild exaggerations—planks in eyes, camels through needles—jolted listeners awake, blending humor with truth. Jesus wasn't just wise; He was wildly engaging.

Why Hyperbole Worked

In Jewish culture, overstatement was an art. Rabbis stretched stories to grab ears, and Jesus perfected it. His hyperbole made truth stick, exposed hypocrisy, and mirrored souls with a laugh.

Greek words like *dokos* (a massive beam) and *kamelos* (Israel's biggest unclean animal) amped up the absurdity. His audience got the joke—and the jab.

The Plank in Your Eye (Matthew 7:3–5)

Imagine a guy stumbling through the market, a construction beam jutting from his eye, trying to flick a speck from his friend's.

It's cartoon-level absurd. The crowd roars. The Pharisees wince.

Jesus nailed self-righteousness: we spot others' flaws while ignoring our own. Humility, not hypocrisy, is the way.

Today's version:
"Mad about your kid's messy room? Check your inbox's 10,000 unread emails first."

Gnats vs. Camels (Matthew 23:24)

The Pharisees obsessed over purity, filtering drinks to avoid a tiny, unclean gnat.

Jesus flipped it:

"You strain out a gnat but swallow a camel!"

Smallest unclean creature versus the biggest—comically absurd.

They nitpicked rules but ignored justice and mercy. The crowd laughed; the point landed.

A Camel Through a Needle's Eye (Matthew 19:24)

To a crowd awed by wealth, Jesus said:

"It's easier for a camel to squeeze through the eye of a needle than for a rich man to enter God's kingdom."

Biggest animal, tiniest hole—jaws dropped, some chuckled.

No narrow gate here; the literal absurdity drove home the truth: you can't buy salvation. Grace is the only way.

Chop Off Hands, Pluck Out Eyes (Matthew 5:29–30)

Preaching to a crowd about sin's seriousness, Jesus said:

"If your eye causes you to sin, gouge it out... better to lose one part than your whole body in hell."

Gasps mixed with nervous laughs.

He wasn't handing out knives—His absurd imagery shocked them into tackling sin radically. Grace saves, but it's not cheap.

Why This Worked

Jesus' hyperbole grabbed ears, flipped perspectives, and stuck like glue.

Years later, the disciples likely retold these stories, laughing:

"Remember the camel bit?"

His humor wasn't just memorable—it transformed hearts.

Picture Jesus at your coffee shop, chuckling:

"Worried about a typo in your email? Better check that camel in your inbox first!"

As His wild humor leaps from the Gospels, what might it teach us about spotting our own planks today?

Next Up: The Sarcasm of Jesus

Buckle up. Jesus didn't just exaggerate—He slung sarcasm like a pro, slicing through pride with a grin.

Chapter 4

Jesus' Parables That Flipped the Script

Wait... The Samaritan Is the Hero?!

Picture yourself in a crowd, hanging on Jesus' every word as He spins a story. Everyone nods—until the ending hits like a thunderbolt.

"The Samaritan is the hero?"
"The tax collector gets God's grace?"

Jesus didn't tell tidy moral tales—His parables were sharp, satirical, and shocking, using irony and surprise to expose hypocrisy and flip cultural norms. This chapter dives into how Jesus' disruptive stories jolted hearts, forcing listeners to rethink everything.

What Is Satire?

Satire uses humor, irony, or exaggeration to expose foolishness and spark truth. Jewish teachers loved it, but Jesus mastered it. His parables weren't just stories—they were divine curveballs, shaking up assumptions with a grin.

The Good Samaritan: The Hero No One Saw Coming (Luke 10:25–37)

A religious expert asks Jesus, **"Who is my neighbor?"** expecting **"Fellow Jews."**

Instead, Jesus tells of a Jewish man attacked and left for dead. A priest passes by—no help. A Levite, another holy man, ignores him.

Then, a Samaritan—despised by Jews—stops, cares, and pays for his recovery.

The crowd gasps; prejudice crumbles. Jesus flips the question, exposing the hypocrisy of those who claim to love God but snub the suffering.

Today's version:
"A pastor walked by, a worship leader ignored him, but the guy nobody respects? He's the hero."

The Pharisee and the Tax Collector: Pride Takes a Fall (Luke 18:9–14)

To self-righteous listeners, Jesus describes two men praying.

A Pharisee brags:

"God, I'm not like sinners—or this tax collector! I fast, I tithe."

The tax collector, a despised traitor, whispers:

"God, have mercy on me, a sinner."

Then the twist: the tax collector, not the Pharisee, goes home right with God.

The crowd's jaws drop. Jesus mocks the Pharisee's performance, showing grace favors the humble.

The Workers in the Vineyard: Unfair Grace (Matthew 20:1–16)

A landowner hires workers—some at dawn, some at noon, some an hour before quitting.

At day's end, all get the same wage. Early workers fume:

"We worked longer!"

The landowner replies:

"Are you envious because I'm generous?"

Jesus' mic-drop:

"The last will be first."

This stings Pharisees who thought they had earned God's favor, revealing grace defies human fairness.

The Mustard Seed: A Tiny Jab at Pride (Matthew 13:31–32)

Jesus says the Kingdom of Heaven is like a mustard seed—tiny, overlooked, but growing into a tree where birds perch.

The crowd chuckles: mustard plants are shrubs, not towering trees, and invasive like weeds.

Jesus' jab mocks elites expecting a grand empire—God's kingdom spreads wildly in humble places.

Why Jesus' Satire Hits Hard

Satire exposed self-righteousness, redefined grace, and made truth linger with a twist.

Imagine Jesus at your church potluck, whispering:

"That guy bragging about his giving? Watch him trip over his pride before dessert."

As His parables flip our expectations, how might His satire reshape our view of grace today?

Next Up: Why Jesus' Humor Still Matters Today

Jesus' humor wasn't just for then—it's for us now. Let's see how.

Chapter 5

Righteousness with a Razor Edge

Jesus vs. the Experts

Picture a pack of Pharisees—Scripture experts with Leviticus memorized—cornering Jesus with a smug theological trap.

Jesus doesn't flinch.

"Have you never read...?" (Mark 2:25)

The crowd buzzes. A disciple stifles a laugh. The Pharisees freeze—did the carpenter's kid just sass them?

Oh, He did, and it was glorious.

I once thought sarcasm was too snarky for holiness, but Jesus wielded it like a scalpel, slicing through pride to reveal truth. His sarcasm wasn't cruel—it was a truth bomb: sharp and unforgettable.

Sarcasm, Bible-Style

Sarcasm—saying the opposite of what you mean—gets a bad rap, but in Scripture, it's a tool.

Elijah mocked Baal's prophets:

"Shout louder—maybe he's napping!" (1 Kings 18:27)

Jesus perfected it, using wit to pop pride, jolt minds, and stump foes with truth.

Let's unpack His sharpest zingers.

"Have You Never Read...?" (Mark 2:25)

When Pharisees nitpick His disciples for plucking grain on the Sabbath, Jesus smirks:

"Have you never read what David did...?"

These guys lived in the Scriptures—they copied them by hand. His Greek word *anaginōskō* (read and understand) stings:

"Oh, experts? Missed that part, huh?"

Jesus shows that rules don't trump mercy, leaving them speechless.

Blasting Hypocrisy: Gnats, Camels, and Loopholes (Matthew 23:16–24; Mark 7:9–13)

Jesus unloads on the Pharisees' obsession with trivial oaths—**"Gold matters, not the temple!"**—and their loopholes, like dodging family duties by claiming money was "for God."

"Nice job ditching God's commands for your traditions!"

He quips, the Greek *kalōs* ("well") dripping irony.

Then, His kicker:

"You blind guides! You strain out a gnat but swallow a camel."

The crowd laughs at the absurd image—filtering tiny insects while gulping the biggest unclean animal. Jesus exposes their focus on rules over justice and love.

"Tell That Fox..." (Luke 13:32)

When Pharisees warn, **"Herod wants to kill You,"** Jesus shrugs:

"Tell that fox I'll keep healing—on the third day, I'll be done."

Calling Herod *alōpēx* (fox) wasn't flattery—it painted him as a sneaky, weak faker.

Jesus' wit shows no earthly power stops God's plan.

"If You Were Blind..." (John 9:39–41)

After healing a blind man, Jesus faces Pharisee scrutiny. He flips it:

"If you were blind, you'd be off the hook. But since you say, 'We see,' your guilt remains."

Pure irony—the blind man sees. The "seeing" Pharisees are clueless. Pride blinds worse than eyes; humility opens them.

Why Sarcasm Worked

Jesus' sarcasm hit like lightning, exposing hypocrisy and redirecting hearts to grace.

Picture Him at your small group, smirking:

"You're debating theology again? Never read the part about love?"

His wit wasn't cruel—it was love with an edge.

As His sarcasm cuts through pride, how might His wit reshape our faith today?

Next Up: Playful Banter with His Disciples

Jesus didn't just sass foes—He teased His friends, too, building bonds with a grin.

Chapter 6

Would Jesus Make You Laugh?

Picture Jesus in the Everyday

Picture Jesus at your local coffee shop, leaning back with a latte, sunlight glinting off His smile. You ask a heavy theological question, bracing for a sermon.

Instead, He quips:

"You're worried about that? Check the plank in your eye first."

You laugh—and the truth clicks.

Jesus wasn't just the greatest teacher; He was the most engaging, joy-filled person ever. His wit, satire, and playful banter weren't just for His time—they're a blueprint for us today.

If Jesus used humor to connect and transform, shouldn't we?

Humor's Power Then and Now

Jesus' humor disarmed doubters, softened hard truths, and made lessons stick. He sassed Pharisees to expose hypocrisy, teased disciples to spark growth, and spun parables to flip assumptions.

Today, that same humor can break barriers and invite honest faith conversations.

Picture Jesus at your office, chuckling:

"Stressed about that deadline? Maybe check the plank in your eye before panicking."

His wit makes truth approachable—whether in sermons, casual chats, or parenting.

Joy Is Holiness

Some see faith as somber, but Jesus overflowed with joy. He celebrated at weddings

(John 2:1–11), welcomed kids who flocked to His warmth (Matthew 19:14), and told His disciples:

"My joy may be in you, complete." (John 15:11)

The most joyful people radiate God's goodness. If faith doesn't spark joy, we might be missing the point.

Living Jesus' Humor

How do we follow His lead?

- **In conversations:** A lighthearted quip—*"Doubts? Even the disciples doubted with Jesus right there!"*—opens hearts.

- **In teaching and parenting:** A funny exaggeration makes truth stick, just like Jesus' camel-through-a-needle image.

- **In our own growth:** Laughing at our flaws keeps us humble, turning conviction into growth with a smile.

But balance is key. Like Jesus, our humor should uplift, not wound—making truth accessible without mocking faith.

Back at the Coffee Shop

Back at the coffee shop, Jesus might lean in, grinning:

"Think you've got faith figured out? Keep reading—there's more joy to find."

His humor wasn't a side note—it revealed a heart full of wisdom and delight.

As His wit fills the Gospels, how might His joy spark yours today?

Final Words: See the Laughing Messiah

If this book has you thinking, **"I never saw Jesus' humor before,"** you're seeing Him anew.

The Gospels brim with wit, irony, and joy. Picture Jesus laughing with you, His joy igniting yours, as you walk forward in faith.

Reread the Gospels. Share this perspective. Live your faith with a smile—because holiness and happiness go hand in hand.

Epilogue

The Science and Scripture of Laughter

Picture Jesus at the Campfire

Picture Jesus at a modern campfire, stars overhead, His laugh warming the night. You ask a deep question, expecting a sermon.

Instead, He quips:

"Still arguing over rules? Try loving like I do—it's funnier."

You chuckle, and truth dawns.

Jesus' humor—His wit, satire, and teasing—wasn't just for then; it's our invitation now.

If He laughed, why don't we talk about laughter more in faith? Scripture and science say holiness and humor are partners, not opposites.

Laughter in Scripture

The Bible brims with joy.

Proverbs 17:22 says:
"A cheerful heart is good medicine,"
a truth science echoes.

In Psalm 2:4, God laughs at human pride from heaven—not cruelly, but with divine perspective.

Ecclesiastes 3:4 declares there is:
"A time to laugh,"
part of God's design for us.

Preaching to a crowd, Jesus promised:
"Blessed are you who weep now, for you will laugh." (Luke 6:21)

Speaking to His disciples, He said:

"My joy may be in you, complete." (John 15:11)

Jesus didn't just teach joy—He lived it.

The Science of Laughter

Science confirms laughter boosts endorphins, cuts stress, and builds bonds—God wired us for joy.

Early Christian art, as scholar Graydon Snyder notes in *Ante Pacem*, shows a smiling Jesus—a truth later art often buried in solemnity.

The early church saw what we sometimes miss: Jesus was a man of joy, not just sorrow.

Laughter as Worship

Back at the campfire, Jesus might grin:

"Think faith's all serious? Laugh with Me—it's holy."

Laughter disarms doubters, softens truth, and keeps us humble, just as Jesus' wit did.

Use it in conversations—a quip like:
"Doubts? Even the disciples doubted with Jesus right there!"
opens hearts.

In teaching or parenting, a funny exaggeration makes faith stick.

But keep it kind, like Jesus—humor should uplift, not wound.

As His laughter echoes through the Gospels, how might His joy spark yours today?

Final Words: The Laughing Messiah

Picture Jesus laughing with you, His joy igniting yours.

Reread the Gospels, spot His wit, share His warmth, and live faith with a smile.

Holiness and humor aren't enemies—they're partners, revealing a Savior who's wise, powerful, and delightfully funny.

Let His joy be your strength—and your invitation to laugh.

About the Author

 Christian A. Dickinson is an author, speaker, and the President & CEO of Learning Engineered Publishing, where he develops faith-based and secular books, including devotionals, children's literature, and educational resources.

With over twenty years as a principal, teacher, and coach, he has shaped the next generation of students and educators—a passion that fuels his writing.

One day, he asked himself: "Was Jesus actually... funny?" That question led him to deep dive into Scripture, history, and early Christian art, where he discovered Jesus wasn't just the greatest teacher of all time. He was also witty, engaging, and unexpectedly funny.

Dickinson's Christian books include *FULL CIRCLE 360: A Devotional for Athletes* and *Micah 6:8: A Prophetic Bridge to Jesus.* He and his wife, Morgan, co-author Christian character-building children's books, including *Fruits of the Spirit for Kids.*

Beyond faith-based work, he publishes STEM magazines, economic literacy books for classrooms, and non-faith-based parenting resources.

When he's not writing, publishing, or mentoring, you can find him debating the best portrayals of Jesus, brainstorming over coffee, or secretly laughing at his own dad jokes.

He believes that if Jesus were here today, He'd still be teaching through humor, flipping tables—and yes, making His disciples laugh along the way.

More by Christian A. Dickinson

I f you enjoyed *Jesus was Funnier Than You Think*, you may also appreciate these Christ-centered resources:

Jesus Was Funnier Than You Think: Unlocking His Wit, Wisdom, and Unexpected Humor
A fresh look at the wit and humor of Jesus Christ — revealing the brilliant, joyful ways He taught truth and disarmed pride.

Every Tear Remembered: God's Presence in Our Grief
A reflection on sorrow, healing, and hope through the lens of God's enduring love.

The Curse of Time: Time Began When Eternity Broke

A theological and personal exploration of time as a consequence of sin—not a neutral part of creation. Drawing from Scripture, Church Fathers, and moments of divine encounter, this book challenges the assumption that time was God's original design and invites readers to rediscover the eternal now of God's presence.

Roar of 'Ēzer: Reclaiming God's Vision for Women's Strength

From Eden's garden to the early church, God named women *'ēzer*—rescuer, strength-bearer, equal partner in His image. This compelling biblical exploration invites women to rise, not as shadows but as co-laborers in God's kingdom. With Scripture, story, and a call to courage, *Roar of 'Ēzer* reveals that women were never meant to shrink. They were always meant to roar.

The Prophetic Equation: Thirty Prophets. One Christ. Zero Coincidence.

An exploration of how thirty prophetic voices across centuries, kingdoms, and crises converge with stunning precision in Jesus Christ —

revealing that Scripture is not random, but a masterpiece of divine design.

Micah 6:8: A Prophetic Bridge to Jesus

A concise biblical commentary exploring how one ancient verse points forward to the life and ministry of Christ.

It's All or Nothing: How Jesus Raised the Standard from Tithing to Full Surrender

A biblical commentary challenging traditional views of tithing by exploring Jesus' call to radical, Spirit-led generosity.

FULL CIRCLE: PREGAME — A Devotional Series for Athletes

Before the whistle blows and the lights come up, PREGAME challenges athletes to prepare their hearts as well as their bodies. With powerful stories, Scripture reflections, and real talk from the locker room, Coach Dickinson and Anthony "Diso" Paradiso equip competitors to lead with faith, play with integrity, and honor Christ in every moment.

Seeing the Humor: A Glossary & Next Steps

Key Terms

Picture Jesus chuckling by the campfire from that night with His disciples (Ch. 1), handing you this glossary to decode His wit:

- **Hyperbole:** Exaggeration to make truth stick, like a camel through a needle's eye (Ch. 3).

- **Satire:** Sharp humor exposing hypocrisy, like mocking Pharisees' camel-swallowing ways (Ch. 4).

- **Rabbinic Humor:** Jewish teachers' playful wordplay and irony, perfected by Jesus' teasing (Ch. 2).

- **Irony:** Saying one thing, meaning another—like **"Have you never read...?"** to know-it-all Pharisees (Ch. 5).

- **Parable:** Short stories with surprise twists, flipping expectations to reveal truth (Ch. 4).

- **Messianic Joy:** Jesus' ministry radiated joy, not just sacrifice, inviting us to laugh (Epilogue).

- **Absurdity in Teaching:** Wild imagery, like planks in eyes, to make spiritual truths unforgettable (Ch. 3).

Recommended Books for Deeper Study

Keep chasing the Laughing Messiah with these:

- **The Humor of Christ** by Elton Trueblood — A classic on Jesus' witty teachings.

- **Between Heaven and Mirth** by James Martin — Joy and humor in faith, perfect for beginners.

- **The Parables of Jesus** by Joachim Jeremias — A deep dive into Jesus' satirical stories.

- **Ante Pacem** by Graydon E. Snyder — Early Christian art showing a smiling Jesus.

- **Jesus Laughed** by Robert Darden — Laughter's role in the Bible, lively and accessible.

- **The Wit and Wisdom of Jesus** by Charles B. Cousar — Jesus' sharp, engaging style.

- **Jesus the King** by Tim Keller — His irony and wisdom through Mark's Gospel.

Why This Matters

Back at that campfire where Jesus teased His disciples (Ch. 1), His quips about planks (Ch. 3), sarcastic jabs at Pharisees (Ch. 5), and satirical parables (Ch. 4) reveal a Savior who taught with joy.

Humor isn't just fun—it deepens faith, breaks barriers, and mirrors God's heart, as science and Scripture confirm (Epilogue).

Reread the Gospels, spot His wit, share His warmth, and live faith with a smile. The Laughing Messiah invites you to see the Good News with fresh eyes—because holiness and humor are partners.

Bible Study Resources

Looking to dive deeper?

We've created a **6-week Bible study** to help you explore the themes of this book in a meaningful and interactive way. Whether studying alone or with a group, this guide will provide Scripture, reflection questions, and action steps to apply what you've learned.

Scan the QR code below to access the complete study guide and additional resources.